YOU CAN YO-YO!

Bruce Weber

Scholastic Inc.

New York   Toronto   London   Auckland   Sydney

ISBN 0-439-08827-5

Copyright © 1998 by Scholastic Inc. All rights reserved. Published by Scholastic Inc. SCHOLASTIC and associated logos are trademarks and/or registered trademarks of Scholastic Inc.

12 11 10 9 8 7 6 5 4 3 2 1   9/9 0 1 2 3 4/0

Printed in the U.S.A.   40

Text design by Laurie Williams

INTRODUCTION

This is the seventy-seventh book I've written for Scholastic. All except two have been about sports. Traditional sports, like football, baseball, basketball.

But last winter an editor asked me to write a new book about yo-yos. I was intrigued. Of course, I had played with yo-yos. They didn't work all that well — or perhaps I wasn't doing it right. Anyway, I soon lost interest. But that was years ago.

Imagine my surprise when I found out that the yo-yo is back, bigger and better than ever. Technology has played a major role. The old wooden yo-yo, with the string attached to the center axle, has given way to plastic and metal. The fixed-axle yo-yo has some stiff competition in new transaxle and ball-bearing yo-yos. Modern yo-yos can sleep for a minute or more, allowing experts to do all sorts of new tricks.

Yo-yo marketing, which began in the late 1920s with Don Duncan, has also reached new heights in the 1990s. Yo-yo contests, which began at candy stores, are now being held in recreation centers and even in big arenas. A yo-yo show in Japan last April packed 40,000 fans into the seats! And TV, of course, helps create new yo-yo enthusiasts all across the United States, Asia, and Europe.

But the biggest surprise is the players themselves. Imagine trying to get Michael Jordan on the phone to talk a little hoop. Or getting Ken Griffey, Jr., on the line to discuss the upcoming American League pennant races. Forget it.

It's a lot different with yo-yo. I called the four national masters. And they all called me back the same day! One national champion, a female teenager in what is still largely a male sport, spent half an hour telling me how she came to turn pro at *age eight*! Unbelievable.

When I started writing this book, I was even invited to the U.S. national championship in Chico, California. It's held there on the first weekend of October every year. Hey, I'm going! It sounds better than the Super Bowl — and you can still get tickets!

This book will clue you in on the latest developments in yo-yo and teach you lots of tricks, from very basic to very tough ones. You'll find tips from the sport's champions, too. I hope you'll have as much fun reading it as I did writing it. And remember — your yo-yo should sleep during your tricks, but you should not!

— *BRUCE WEBER*

LIFE'S UPS AND DOWNS

Chances are you've played with a yo-yo. (Otherwise, you wouldn't have picked up this book!)

Well, join the crowd. Unlike most sports, which are popular in one place but not another, yo-yo is truly international. In most of Europe, for example, nobody knows or cares whether the Yankees or Braves or Dodgers are the World Series baseball champions. And even Michael Jordan isn't a folk hero all over the globe.

But yo-yo. That's something else. While the first baseball World Series was held in 1903, and the first Super Bowl was played in 1967, yo-yos date back thousands of years.

Most history books say yo-yos were invented in China. They were made of two wooden disks with a wide space between them. A string was knotted to a shank joining the two disks, so all the yo-yo could do was go up and down. Forget Walking the Dog or Shooting the Moon.

Yo-yos made of wood, metal, and stone were also popular in ancient Greece. In fact, on one piece of pottery in an Athens museum there is a picture of a young man playing with a yo-yo. According to historians, the pottery is about 2,500 years old.

The yo-yo wasn't really popular in Europe, though, until the late 1700s. Then, yo-yos became the favorite toys of the royal families of England and France. If you visit the British Museum in London, you'll see a two-hundred-year-old painting of the Prince of Wales playing with a yo-yo. As a result, yo-yos were often called "the Prince of Wales's toy." They were also called quizzes or bandalores.

The French refused to be outdone. The son of Marie Antoinette and King Louis XVI was also a big yo-yo fan. So were many French noblemen, who owned yo-yos made of ivory and other expensive materials.

But the yo-yo we know today can be traced to the Philippines. Legend has it that as far back as the 1500s, Filipino soldiers were using versions of today's yo-yos as weapons. Of course, they were a lot larger than modern yo-yos — the string was replaced with heavy rope, sometimes as long as 20 feet. But gradually the yo-yo turned into a toy. Filipino fathers carved yo-yos out of fine wood or animal horns. It didn't take long before almost every child in the Philippines was playing with a yo-yo.

Even the name yo-yo started there. In Tagalog, the native language of the Philippines, the word for comeback is — you've got it — yo-yo.

The yo-yo eventually made its way to the United States. But it took a long while for it to become popular. The first U.S. patent for yo-yos was awarded in 1866 to two Ohio inventors who called their toy a "better bandalore," using the old English name. Through the next decades, more and more patents were filed. One man owned a patent for a bandalore made of hard India rubber, like a hockey puck. Somebody patented a one-piece bandalore, and someone else registered a bandalore made with removable bells. One inventor believed that wooden bandalores were hazardous to the health of young yo-yoists. So he got a license to make glass bandalores. Believe it or not, a patent was even awarded to a man who wanted to make a bandalore that, except for the string, was entirely edible! Imagine doing that to a football!

THE YO-YO YEARS

Yo-yos finally took off in the United States with the help of a man named Pedro Flores. In 1927, he worked in the dining room of a hotel in Santa Monica, California. He loved to spend his spare time whittling yo-yos — they had been his favorite toys when he was growing up in the Philippines. And once he made them, he played with them, much to the amusement of some of the guests at the hotel.

They asked him to make yo-yos for them. Pedro Flores was happy to do it.

The guests took Flores's yo-yos home. Before he knew it, Flores was getting requests for the toy from all over the country.

Within a couple of years, he was in business. He opened the Flores Yo-Yo Corporation and began shipping his products to customers everywhere. Yo-yos were hot in Los Angeles as well as in San Francisco. Folks in Denver and Dallas and New Orleans loved yo-yos. And yo-yo fever also moved into the big cities in the Northeast.

To promote his yo-yo, Flores hired other Filipinos to tour the country demonstrating the old "new" toy. Yo-yo contests began, but nobody did tricks in them. The contests were tests of endurance.

While Flores was cranking out yo-yos in Los Angeles, the most important step in the yo-yo revolution was taking place in San Francisco. Somebody showed a yo-yo to a businessman named Donald Duncan. It wasn't a Flores yo-yo, because all it could do was go up and down. (Flores's yo-yos had a nonfixed string, so they could sleep.) Still, Duncan was fascinated, and he began to research the new toy.

Eventually, he met Pedro Flores and bought his company. Duncan opened a factory in Chicago and began turning out Flores yo-yos. Within a year, he was calling them Duncan yo-yos, and a great American tradition was underway. The brilliant Duncan made other advances, too. He rounded and smoothed the outer edges of the yo-yo so that they wouldn't hurt the yo-yoist's hand when the toy came spinning back. Duncan also developed a new string that wouldn't unravel or break very often. It was so smooth that the yo-yo would spin longer, and the yo-yoist could perform more difficult tricks.

Duncan hired Flores and his friends to demonstrate the Duncan yo-yo. They were called Duncan Yo-Yo Professionals, and they toured the country, teaching young people the newest tricks. Duncan gave memorable names to the tricks — that's where Walk the Dog and Rocking the Baby started. And he started the first Duncan yo-yo contests. These contests crowned state and city champions. Youngsters competed hard to win the big prize, a sweater with an emblem that read DUNCAN YO-YO WINNER! Later, the prizes increased in value and often included bicycles, trips to exotic places, even cash.

The yo-yo was on its way.

Duncan worked with newspapers around the country to publicize his contests. The famous publisher William Randolph Hearst was one of the first to jump on the Duncan bandwagon. When Duncan showed Hearst that yo-yos could sell newspapers (contestants had to sell subscriptions to qualify for the contests), Hearst had many of his papers participate. There's a famous ad for a Duncan yo-yo championship in Chicago, signed — believe it or not — by the yo-yo editor of Hearst's *Chicago Herald-Examiner*.

Well-known politicians, actors, actresses, and ballplayers had their pictures taken playing with Duncan yo-yos. Bing Crosby, one of America's top popular singers, sang a yo-yo song. A well-promoted yo-yo contest in a fairly large city could sell millions of yo-yos. The yo-yo craze had begun.

The canny Duncan knew he had the world on a string. He repeated the yo-yo's American success in Europe, using the same promotional techniques. He sent demonstrators all over the Continent. The yo-yo fascinated Europeans, particularly the French. Even people vacationing along the French Riviera played with yo-yos. One Duncan yo-yo contest ended when a yo-yo slipped out of a competitor's hand and conked one of the judges on the head, knocking him out. Not to be outdone by the Americans, the French also wrote a yo-yo song. The little Filipino toy had taken over the world.

Why was the yo-yo so popular? Maybe it was because the yo-yo craze happened during the Great Depression. Few people had much money. But it didn't take a lot of money to play yo-yo. Duncan had three major models. The first, a junior yo-yo, cost a nickel. The beginner's

Return Top cost a dime.

And the top-of-the-line model cost only a quarter. The No. 77 Tournament Yo-Yo was made of fine northern hard maple wood. It was the yo-yo that every aspiring champion had to have. And then you only needed to buy two more things. The top strings came in a little clear bag and were two for five cents. And, for a dime, you could buy the official book that showed all of the tricks. With that tiny investment, the yo-yoist had everything he or she needed. And that was probably one of the reasons for the yo-yo's success.

The yo-yo stayed hot until the start of World War II. Then, because it was wartime, the Duncan Company couldn't easily get the lumber it needed to make yo-yos — and it didn't try very hard to get it, either. The company cut out the contests and the demonstration tours, and newspapers didn't have space to promote them in any case.

Realizing he needed to improve production, Duncan decided to move into a new factory — in Luck, Wisconsin. It became the unofficial world yo-yo headquarters. But as Donald Duncan would later admit, "It was too far away from the action."

By the late 1950s, the Duncan Company was in big trouble. Sales were down, expenses were up. The company decided that TV advertising would solve the problem. The investment paid off — too well. Sales zoomed quickly from around $650,000 a year to nearly $7 million a year. The factory worked around the clock. Labor costs zoomed ahead of the sales numbers. Duncan fell behind filling orders and had to use expensive air shipments to make deadlines. In spite of the yo-yo's popularity, Duncan was losing money.

Then Don Duncan spent a fortune on a court case. He was trying to prevent other companies from calling their toys yo-yos. But the court decided that the word yo-yo applied to any spinning-top toy and not just to Duncan's toys. Shortly afterward, the company went bankrupt — and out of business.

The Duncan name was bought by Flambeau Plastics. Flambeau still makes Duncan yo-yos, but they're all plastic now. They sell dozens of other brands, too.

And the days when Duncan Yo-Yo Professionals could be found at candy stores everywhere, distributing patches to young yo-yoists and performing tricks, were gone forever.

JUST DO IT!

Yo-yos come in many sizes but only a couple of shapes. The traditional yo-yo looks like a sliced bagel — the two halves are separated by the yo-yo axle, the thing the string is wound around. The butterfly yo-yo is a variation of the traditional shape — the two halves of the sliced bagel are attached the wrong way, so they look like they're upside

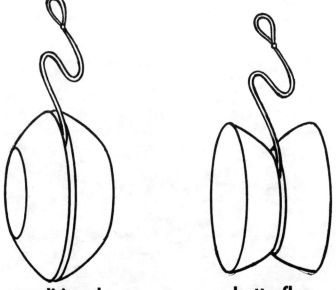

traditional   **butterfly**

down. The butterfly yo-yo helps some tricks work more smoothly.

A loop of string is tied around the axle of most yo-yos. When the yo-yo "sleeps," it stops going up and down and just spins around on this loop. A fixed-axle yo-yo can't sleep at all, because the string is permanently glued to one spot on the axle. But the new transaxle yo-yo can sleep for up to a full minute — its string is guided by tiny ball bearings. Lots of new tricks have been developed for transaxle yo-yos. But they are forbidden in some yo-yo competitions.

Here's how to get ready to yo-yo, no matter what kind of yo-yo you have.

Make sure that your string is the right length. With the yo-yo resting on the floor, the string should be about as high as your belly button. Cut it there. If the string is too long, the yo-yo will bang on the floor when you use it. If it's too short, you might have trouble doing some tricks.

Next, check that the string isn't too loose

or too tight around the axle. If it is, it won't be able to sleep. You can loosen or tighten your string easily. Simply stick a pen or pencil tip inside your yo-yo. Then, catch the loop with it. To loosen the loop, pull it farther away from the axle. To make it tighter, pull it closer to the axle. Some yo-yos come apart. If yours is this kind, you can make the same adjustments by hand.

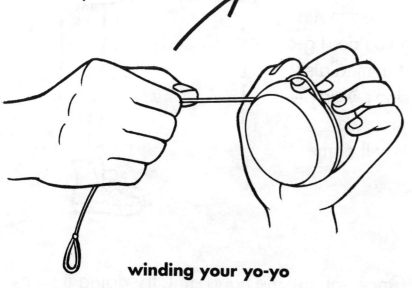

winding your yo-yo

Now wind the string around the yo-yo. Put your finger on the opening between the two halves of the yo-yo, and wind the string

away from you a few times over your finger and around the yo-yo. Then, remove your finger, pull the string tight around the axle, and wind until only an inch or two of string remains.

Tie a slipknot at the top of the string, and place it just past the first knuckle on your middle finger. If you practice enough, it may get very tight. That's OK. In fact, expert yo-yoists often develop a callus right there. Then, hold the yo-yo in the palm of your hand with the string stretching down the rest of your finger and over the yo-yo's axle. Usually, you'll need to flip the yo-yo from this position, keeping your palm facing you.

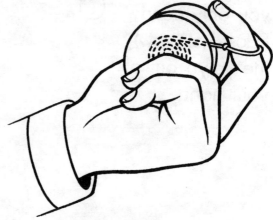

starting position

Let's start with the most basic of all tricks, the **Gravity Pull**. Like many tricks, this one requires you to toss the yo-yo from your palm and over your fingers, keeping your palm facing you. With the Gravity Pull, you only need to toss (not throw) the yo-yo out of your hand.

Just before the string unwinds all the way, pull or jerk your hand toward you, and the yo-yo will return to the top. Catch it in the same position you' started with. If you don't get it immediately, don't worry — practice. It will come.

Once you get the hang of it, try doing it many times in a row. Don't catch the yo-yo. Let it hit your hand, go back down, and pull it back. That's called dribbling the yo-yo.

Next you need to learn the **Power Throw**, a basic step in many other tricks. Again, the yo-yo is in your hand; your palm is facing you.

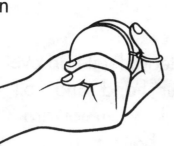

Now raise your hand and elbow until the yo-yo is almost even with your ear. Then quickly bring your hand down in front of you, letting the yo-yo go as you begin your downward motion. As in the Gravity Pull, the yo-yo leaves your hand over the tips of your fingers.

But this time you should stop your hand just above your waist and turn it over. (Make sure you don't do that until the yo-yo has left your hand.) With your palm now down, catch the yo-yo when it returns. To get the hang of this, try practicing without a yo-yo: lift your wrist and elbow up, pretend to throw, and turn your hand over. In both the Gravity Pull and the Power Throw, you must train yourself not to jerk the yo-yo up too soon or too late. It should have time to get all the way to the bottom of the string before you pull it back.

Now you're ready to **Hop the Fence**. The key to this trick is a good Power Throw. The difference? Turn your hand over, but don't catch the yo-yo when it comes up.

Instead, let it hop over your hand and roll back down toward the bottom of its string. Finally, bring the yo-yo back up to your hand. Make sure you throw the yo-yo hard enough at first for it to come back at the end of this trick.

To do the **Forward Pass**, start by holding the yo-yo as in all the tricks above. Then, move your arm behind your back. Bring your arm back in front of you, as if you were beginning to throw a bowling ball. As you do so, let go of your yo-yo. It will roll off your fingers, fly in front of you, and then return to your hand. At the end of this trick, your hand should be in the same position it started out in — palm facing up. Some common mistakes in the Forward Pass are grabbing the yo-yo when your hand starts forward, bending your wrist so your hand will stay level until it's out front, or turning your hand on the forward swing.

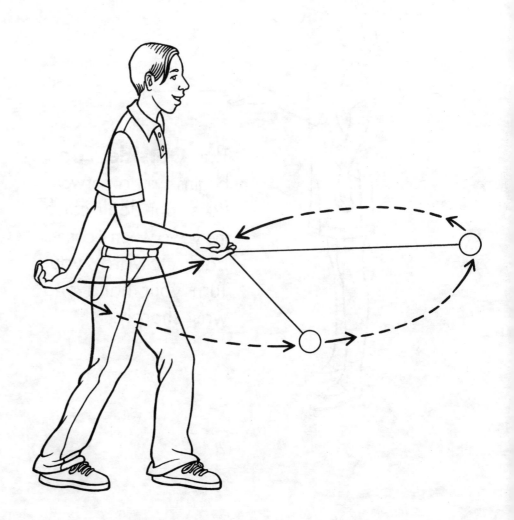

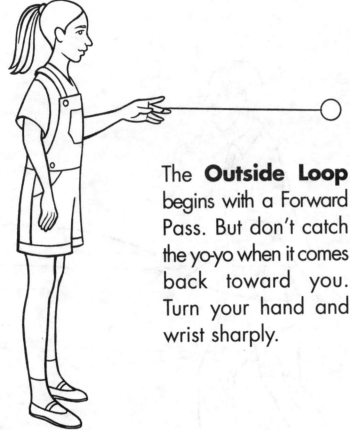

The **Outside Loop** begins with a Forward Pass. But don't catch the yo-yo when it comes back toward you. Turn your hand and wrist sharply.

Your hand should face inward and your wrist outward, allowing the yo-yo to circle your hand on the outside of the wrist. With another flick of your wrist, send it back to the end of the string for another Forward Pass. Only then should it return to your hand. The key to this trick is a good Forward Pass at the start. Keep your hand low. If you lift it high, it will be hard to catch the yo-yo.

If you can get the Outside Loop, the **Inside Loop** shouldn't be much harder. It's exactly the same — except you flick your wrist in the opposite direction and the yo-yo circles on the inside of your wrist before it goes out into another Forward Pass.

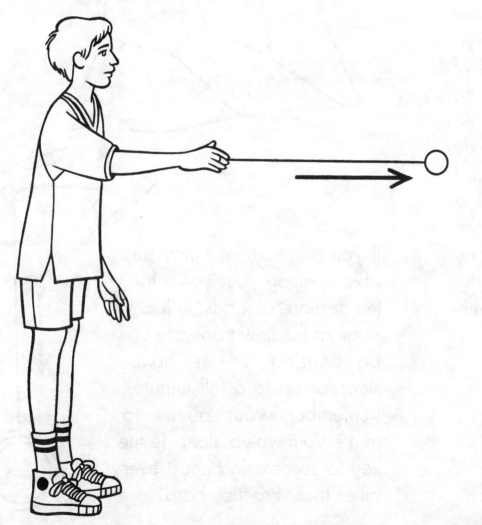

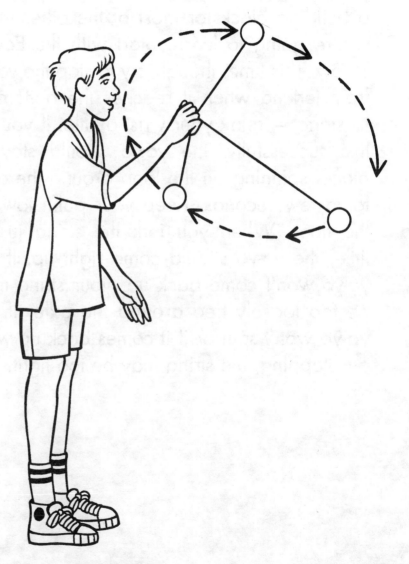

Now you're ready to learn the **Sleeper** (sometimes also called the **Spinner**). This is a building block for most of the other tricks you're going to learn. Start with the Power Throw. This time, though, try to stop the yo-yo from jerking when it reaches the bottom of its string — relax your wrist a little. If you do this successfully, the yo-yo should stay in place, spinning on the loop around the axle for a few seconds. Keep your palm toward the floor. When you jerk the string just a little, the yo-yo should come right up. If the yo-yo won't come back up, your string may be too loosely tied around the axle. If the yo-yo won't spin or if it comes back up without stopping, the string may be too tight.

If you practice, you may be able to sleep your yo-yo for ten or more seconds. In fact, some of the new transaxle or ball-bearing yo-yos have slept for up to a full minute. Remember, your ability to make your yo-yo sleep is the key to success in almost every other trick. Practice hard!

Now you should be ready to do some spinning tricks. Many of these were on the original list of tricks in the Duncan yo-yo contests. And they're still the basic tricks of the sport.

First you're going to **Walk the Dog**. Make the yo-yo sleep, then gently lower it to the floor.

The **Creeper** begins just like Walk the Dog. Start with a Sleeper and then lower your yo-yo to the floor. Then bend down on your knee, lowering your hand to the floor. Finally, give the yo-yo a slight pull. It will start creeping back to you.

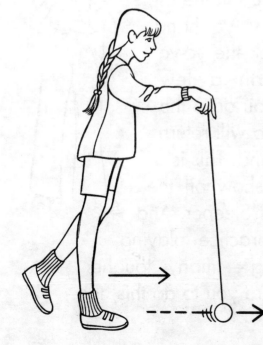

Next walk it out in front of you — like a dog on a leash. Don't let the string go limp. Make a small upward wrist jerk to bring the yo-yo back to your hand. See how long you can make it walk.

The **Dragster** is another variation on Walk the Dog. Before you begin, make sure your yo-yo has some room to travel — and make sure nobody is in its way! Throw a hard Sleeper and then begin to work the loop off your finger.

One more basic trick you can do with the Sleeper is the **Pendulum**. Again, throw a nice fast Sleeper. Then, with your other hand, grab the yo-yo string about five inches above the yo-yo.

As your yo-yo continues to sleep, lower it to the floor — and then let go! The yo-yo should zoom out in front of you like a runaway racing car.

Move the hand that's holding the string high up in the air, keeping your yo-yo hand down low. Rock the yo-yo back and forth a few times. When you drop the string, the yo-yo will return right to your hand. This is a good way to show off the strength of your Sleeper. And it's good to practice playing with the string — many tougher tricks will require you to do this, too.

Once you've mastered these tricks, you're ready to tackle some tougher ones. Try the **Breakaway** first. Your objective in this trick is to get the yo-yo from shoulder-high on one side of your body to shoulder-high on the other. Begin with your elbow at shoulder level and pointing out, as if you were showing off your muscles! Release your yo-yo, then bring your elbow down sharply. The yo-yo will fly out and down and begin to sleep.

Then swing your arm a c r o s s the front of your body and toward your other shoulder. The yo-yo will follow your arm, but first it will hesitate for a second, appearing to hang in thin air. Finally, bring it back to your hand. The key to success is to throw the yo-yo out, not down, on the release.

Around the World is another famous trick. Throw the yo-yo from your shoulder, as you did in Breakaway. This time, though, don't pull the yo-yo back to your hand when it reaches your other shoulder. Instead, let it go over your shoulder and do a complete circle around you. Try to get the yo-yo to remain at the end of the string through the whole trick. And be careful when you do Around the World. It takes lots of room. Make sure there's no one around you when you try it!

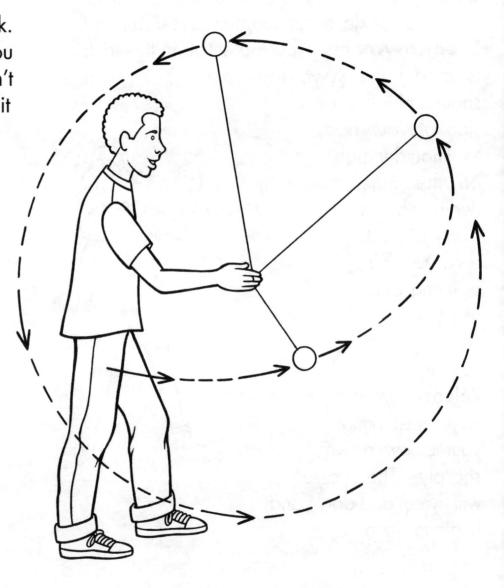

① Once you can go Around the World, you can attempt **Around the Corner**. Throw a fast Sleeper.

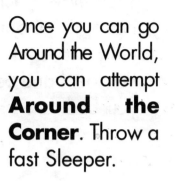

② Then raise your hand to the scout's oath position. Bring the yo-yo around your elbow so it's behind your arm. (Don't let it get behind your shoulder. Keep your elbow high.)

③ The string should hang over your arm. Then lower your hand (the one holding the yo-yo), and grab the string just above the yo-yo with your thumb and index finger.

④ Quickly jerk it upward. The yo-yo will move up the string and over your arm. It will then drop in front of you. Now you can pull it back to your hand like you did in the Gravity Pull.

Now you can try **Rock the Baby**. This is the most basic — and the most popular — of all string tricks. (String tricks are like the cat's cradle tricks you can do with a plain old loop of string.) You'll need to be able to sleep the yo-yo for about seven or eight seconds to Rock the Baby correctly. Throw a fast Sleeper.

1
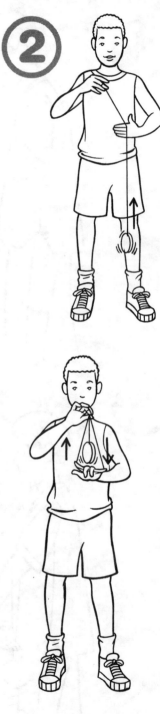

Then move your yo-yo hand to about chest height in front of you. Put your hand between your body and the yo-yo.

2

4

Now you'll see a loop. Spread the fingers of your non yo-yo hand through the loop and pull down to form the "cradle." Let the yo-yo, sleeping all the while, rock easily inside the cradle. When the yo-yo stops sleeping, release the string. The yo-yo will return for you to catch.

Caution: Be prepared to untie all sorts of knots in the string until you really learn how to Rock the Baby. You might want to practice with a "dead" (not sleeping) yo-yo first.

3

Then, with your yo-yo hand, grab the string several inches above the yo-yo.

To **Skin the Cat**, throw another hard Sleeper.

When you drop your hand, it will fly out into a Forward Pass.

Then run the index finger of your other hand up the string until it's about 8 inches from the spinning yo-yo. Then, push the yo-yo up and out. It should pivot around your finger and toward you.

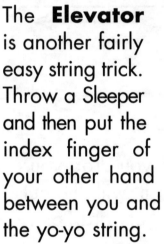

The **Elevator** is another fairly easy string trick. Throw a Sleeper and then put the index finger of your other hand between you and the yo-yo string.

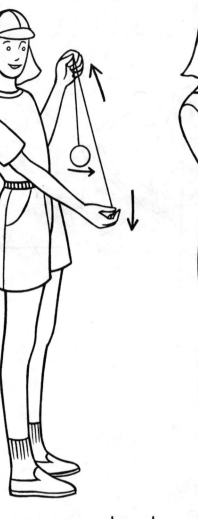

Bring your yo-yo hand down and then, with all four fingers, grab the string right above the yo-yo.

Pull your other hand out of the loop now. You should be left holding the yo-yo string right above the yo-yo with your yo-yo hand. Drop the string with your right hand. The yo-yo will fall down and then come right back up.

You don't have to wait until Saint Patrick's Day to try the **Three-Leaf Clover**. This is a three-part trick. Throw the yo-yo up and out in front of you as if you are doing a very high Forward Pass. As the yo-yo returns, flick your wrist to the inside. The yo-yo should go out again, right in front of you. It will make another loop. As the yo-yo comes back, flick your wrist again. Again the yo-yo should go inside your arm — this time, direct it toward the floor. That's the clover's stem. Finally, jerk your wrist to make the yo-yo come back for your catch.

For the **Flying Saucer**, you start again as if you're flexing your muscle. You'll need to make the yo-yo spin, but you'll have to throw it down and sideways across your body. To do that, you'll need to throw the yo-yo on an angle, more sideways than straight up.

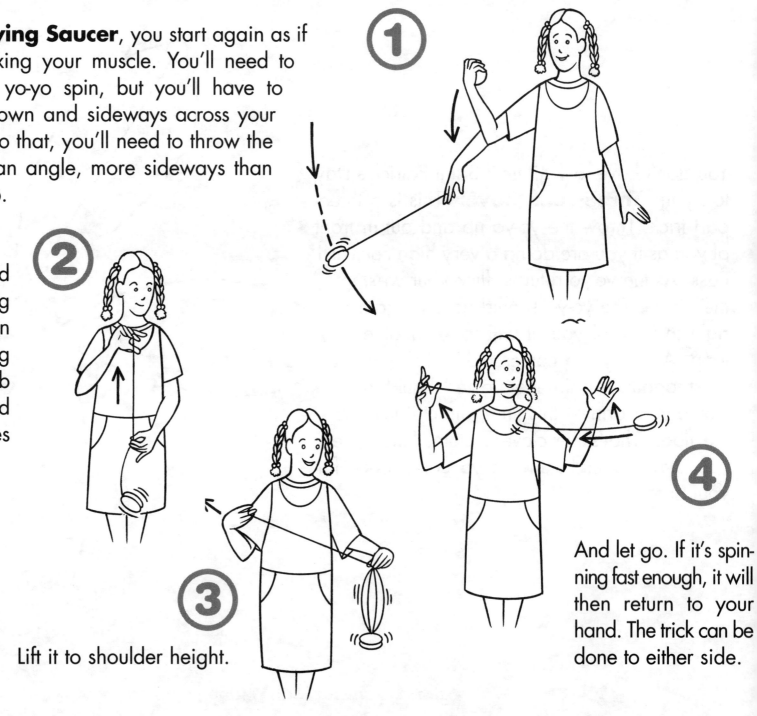

The yo-yo should now be spinning on its side. Then grab the string with the thumb of your free hand about 6 inches from the yo-yo.

Lift it to shoulder height.

And let go. If it's spinning fast enough, it will then return to your hand. The trick can be done to either side.

1

The **Man on the Flying Trapeze** is a crowd-pleasing trick. Begin as you did for the Breakaway, throwing the yo-yo from shoulder level, bringing your elbow down sharply.

2

The yo-yo should start to rise. Then place the index finger of your other hand so that the string swings over it.

3

The yo-yo should then land on the extended string about one or two lengths from your finger.

4

Now, keeping the yo-yo sleeping, let it glide back and forth on the string.

5

Finally, lift the string with the same index finger and pull it away. Now flip the yo-yo up. It should return to your hand. You'll need to practice hard to learn how to land the yo-yo on the string.

① ② ③

By this time, you're probably ready for some more difficult tricks. Start with the **Brain Twister**. You need to start with a fast Sleeper. Now move your opposite index finger forward and onto the string.

Lift it straight up so the yo-yo hangs midway between your hands, about chest high.

Then with your yo-yo hand, insert the string inside the yo-yo. Use the same finger to take the now-doubled string toward your body.

Bring the other hand for-ward and down. The yo-yo should swing up, over, and down.

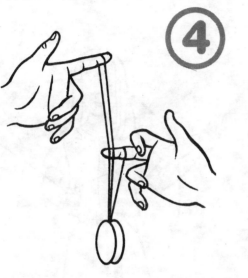

4

You're almost there now. Use your yo-yo hand to bring the yo-yo toward you. At the same time, move your other finger — and the string — the other way. This will make the yo-yo reverse, going up, around, and off the opposite hand's index finger.

5

The yo-yo will then unwind, and you should catch it out in front of you.

6

If you like Around the World, you'll probably like the **Pinwheel**, too. It starts, like most tricks, with a strong Sleeper.

Then spin the yo-yo three times around your finger. Finally, drop the yo-yo. It should come back to your hand.

Now use your opposite hand to pick up the yo-yo by the string fairly close to the yo-yo.

Shoot the Moon is one of the most difficult tricks. It starts out with a Forward Pass.

As the yo-yo starts to return, jerk your wrist outward to toss the yo-yo upward. Just past the midpoint of its return trip, give it another hard forward toss. That will send the yo-yo out in front of you. See how many of these you can do without stopping!

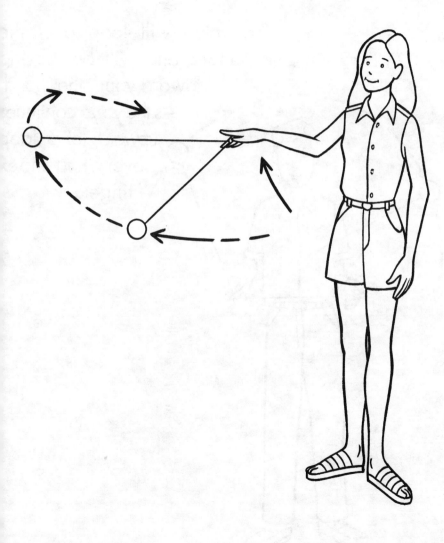

Are you ready to go for **Double or Nothing**? Begin as you would for the Breakaway. As the yo-yo reaches its full extension, take the index finger of your opposite hand and put it on the string at about the midpoint.

The yo-yo will loop over the finger and will be moving toward your other hand. As the yo-yo continues upward, let it loop over that index finger.

Then let the yo-yo come back to hit the index finger of your other hand. Now it will loop back under that finger, toward your yo-yo hand again. That's the double in Double or Nothing. Land the yo-yo on either of the string segments as in the Man on the Flying Trapeze. Want to get the yo-yo back? Flip it gently off the string, and pull both fingers out of the loops. The yo-yo will drop down, allowing you to jerk it back up to your hand. Once you've got this figured out, can **Triple or Nothing** be far behind?

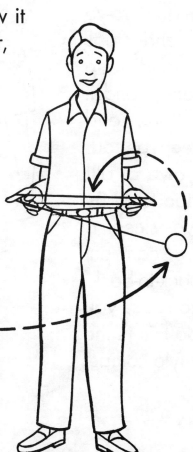

Now you're ready for a two-part trick. When the yo-yo finishes sleeping and starts its return to your hand, loop it around your hand, send it back to the bottom, and begin another sleep period. Don't catch the yo-yo at all! Why is this so important? By making the yo-yo sleep a second time, you can put tricks together back-to-back. In major yo-yo contests, you must be able to do this in the all-important freestyle competition.

Start with the **Warp Drive**. This trick combines the Inside Loop and Around the World. Begin with the Forward Pass, snapping the yo-yo inward as it passes your hand.

Take it into a forward Around the World.

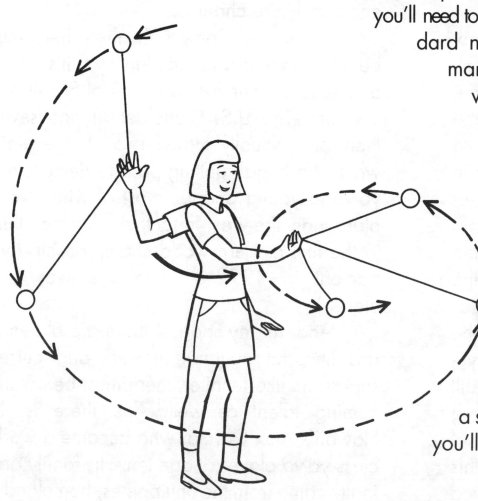

And whip it again as it passes your hand. Eventually you'll need to go Around the World three times, the standard number in competition. This is only one of many two-part tricks. If you've gotten this far without much trouble, you're well on your way to yo-yo success. How many tricks are there altogether? Hundreds. But they all really start with the ones you've learned here.

When you feel comfortable with these, you might even want to start on two-handed tricks. While many competitions feature both one-handed and two-handed championships, most of the experts consider only two-handed players the real champs. You'll have to get a second yo-yo, of course. But with two yo-yos, you'll have double the fun!

YO-YO: IT'S BACK!

What makes a sport successful? It's people. In baseball, Yankee Stadium is known as the House That Ruth Built. That nickname salutes Babe Ruth, the Yankee star of the 1920s and 1930s who brought the fans to the ballpark. They don't salute equipment in any sport's hall of fame. They honor the great players who made the game famous.

That's the way it is in yo-yo, too. In the yo-yo set, the household names are the national masters, four men in their fifties who've been associated with yo-yo since the late 1950s. Call them the Babe Ruths of yo-yo. Each of them — Dale Oliver and Bill deBoisblanc of San Francisco, Dale Myrberg of Salt Lake City, and Dennis McBride of Buellton, California — is a superstar in his own right. And though they've competed against one another for decades, there's no real rivalry among them. In fact, you're likely to find several of them together at any time, bringing the message of yo-yo to young audiences of future champs.

If there's a Babe Ruth, then there must be a Michael Jordan, too. In yo-yo, it's national champion Jennifer Baybrook of St. Albans, Vermont. The U.S. titleholder at age seventeen, she actually turned pro at age eight, when she began getting paid to demonstrate yo-yo to young people, most of whom were older than she was. In fact, she finished third in the first modern world championship tournament in 1992 — when she was only eleven!

And, in any sport, if there are old veterans like the national masters and current superstars like Jennifer, there must be up-and-coming talent as well. And there is. It's Hawaii's Alex Garcia, who became a world-class yo-yo player at age ten. His family originally came from the Philippines, homeland of the original yo-yo superstars.

How did the great yo-yo players get their start? Some of the game's superstars share their stories here.

DALE OLIVER

A native of Kansas City, Dale was born in 1940. Like so many other youngsters, he was given an inexpensive Duncan yo-yo to play with. (Remember, those were the days when Duncan was sending its Duncan Yo-Yo Professionals to toy and candy stores everywhere, running all sorts of neighborhood contests.)

The contests turned Dale onto yo-yo big-time. He got interested in the sport and started learning new tricks. Then he quickly became a champion, capturing one Duncan contest at age twelve and two more in the two following years. When he showed up for the contest the fourth year, the pro invited Dale to drop out of the contest. "Would you

like to do this for money?" he asked.

"I didn't hesitate for a minute," Dale remembers. So he started working for Duncan, performing, teaching, and running contests at dime stores for two to three hours a day after school and on Saturdays. "It was a lot of fun," he says.

By age seventeen, he was working full-time for the yo-yo company. "It was exciting. We'd go to one area for eight weeks at a time, doing our thing. Then we'd move to another town. I did that until I was twenty-four. That was about the time Duncan went bankrupt."

It looked like that might be the end of Dale's yo-yo career. But then Flambeau bought the Duncan name and started making Duncan yo-yos out of plastic. Yo-yos became a trend again in the late 1960s.

"Flambeau called me in 1969, and I went back into the yo-yo business, making personal appearances all over until 1974," says Dale. "Later on, I heard from Don

Duncan, Jr., the son of Don Duncan, who started the whole thing. He had come up with a new rim-weighted yo-yo and needed my help. I went to work designing yo-yos and found it fascinating."

And now, approaching age sixty, Dale is busier than ever. In February 1989, he began doing school programs, teaching yo-yo fun and safety, and selling yo-yos. Parent-Teacher Associations at each school sponsored the programs, raising funds by sharing in the profits of the yo-yo sales.

The Pacific Science Center in Seattle, which was preparing a special program on things that spin, asked Dale if he could use the yo-yo to teach science. "No problem," said Dale, who produced a physics lesson called the Science of Spin.

"I'm still doing it," says Dale. "And I'm training others to teach it, too. It's both entertaining and educational."

Perhaps Dale's greatest contribution to the current yo-yo craze is the world championship. From 1932 to 1992, England's Harvey Lowe was the reigning world yo-yo champ. That's because no world championships were held for sixty years! Dale arranged to bring back the tournament.

Dale went to Montreal to serve as the judge and was somehow persuaded to enter the contest. So he taught the best-ever female yo-yo player, Linda Sengpiel, how to judge. Then he became one of the twenty-two contestants, and he won, finally succeeding the long-forgotten Lowe as world champ.

Dale is thrilled to see how yo-yo has grown over the past few years. "It's a combination of technology and marketing," he says. Transaxle yo-yos, in which only the outside ring touches the string, are extremely popular. These yo-yos can sleep longer, sometimes as long as a minute, allowing young players to learn more easily and to do all sorts of new tricks. "That's one of the major reasons why the yo-yo growth curve really jumped ahead in 1996, and we haven't looked back."

The growth has been worldwide, too. When Dale and the other U.S. national masters appeared at National Yo-Yo Day in Japan in April 1998, more than 40,000 spectators packed a Tokyo stadium.

"The availability of yo-yo videos has really aided the boom," Dale says. "The first one, called Vide-Yo, appeared in the early 1980s, and now there are dozens." Many yo-yo manufacturers have produced their own videos. Tommy Smothers, a great yo-yo enthusiast who uses the yo-yo in his comedy act, also has one. But Dale, not surprisingly, recommends his own — and those done by Dennis McBride.

"I suggest that youngsters learn the twenty-eight tricks used in American Yo-Yo Association competitions from my videos," says Dale. "Then they should add Dennis's, which are great for two-handed routines with both front mounts and side mounts."

DENNIS MCBRIDE

Dale Oliver has spent most of his adult life involved with yo-yos, but national master Dennis McBride has answered to a higher calling. He is a full-time Christian minister. But he hasn't been far away from yo-yo. "I've been using the yo-yo to help teach goal setting and antidrug lessons to schoolchildren," says Dennis.

Like many of the sport's superstars, Dennis started early. One of his neighbors was the California state girls' champion. She and a few other youngsters taught Dennis some of the basic tricks. "I probably took it a little more seriously than the rest," he says. He quickly began winning local Duncan contests and continued to dominate until the mandatory retirement age (at that time) of fifteen.

When he finished his religious training in 1988, Dennis called the Duncan folks for an update on his sport. They hired him to train college students and perform promotions at Disneyland. Dennis has never competed in the world championships that began in 1992. "When the worlds first started, they weren't nearly as big as they are now," Dennis says. "And I really didn't want to compete against some of the kids I'd taught. The world title has a certain commercial value. But the national master title gives me all the prestige I need. It's really the highest honor in the sport."

These days, Dennis is traveling and promoting yo-yo everywhere. He's involved in Alan Nagale's High Performance demonstrating team and in making yo-yo commercials. He spends some time in Japan, where the Bandai Corporation, the world's third largest toy maker, has turned yo-yo into the hottest sport. "Yo-yo is really getting hot elsewhere in Asia and in Europe, too. It's tremendously exciting," says Dennis.

DALE MYRBERG

Dale Myrberg is excited, too. He has finally retired from Utah Power, the utility company, where he was a senior project sponsor.

Now he's into yo-yo full-time. Like the other national masters, Dale started young. "I was only five or six when my brother brought me home a pink-and-white Duncan," Dale remembers. "I was so small, I had to stand on a chair to make it work properly."

Dale was around ten years old when his interest in yo-yo really took off. "There was a Duncan contest at Jimmy Doyle's store across from Jefferson Elementary School. That got me going," he says. By the time he was thirteen he was hired as a Duncan demonstrator, which, he says, "eliminated me from competition. But I made a deal to enter again at age fifteen, so I could beat my friends for the unofficial state championship."

Again, like so many of the older champions, he retired after that. But he picked it up again in his early thirties when his buddies on a surveyor crew challenged him. "I told them I had been a yo-yo champ as a kid, and they didn't believe me," he says. "We got a couple of Duncan Satellites, and that got me started again."

Yo-yo success came fairly quickly after that. Word of Dale's ability spread, and he became a highly sought-after entertainer in Utah. He did Duncan promotions and school assemblies. With the help of Brad Countryman, he landed a couple of spots on *The Smothers Brothers Comedy Hour*. Tommy Smothers is known as Yo-Yo Man and, according to Dale, "is a pretty good one-handed yo-yoist."

In fact, Dale credits Tommy Smothers as a major factor in the current yo-yo boom. And Dale's part of it, too. He frequently performs in a clownlike costume with a flashing tie and baggy Dockers, which enable him to do all sorts of in-the-pocket tricks.

Dale is an old-fashioned yo-yoist. "I use fixed-axle wood yo-yos. I'm not a big fan of the new transaxle ball-bearing models." And his approach must be working: Dale's 1998 travel schedule included demonstrations in Japan and Australia, with stops throughout the United States as well.

JENNIFER BAYBROOK

If the national masters are the hall of famers of yo-yo, then teenager Jennifer Baybrook of St. Albans, Vermont, is the sport's Michael Jordan. In a sport dominated by men and boys, young Jennifer has been prominent on the world yo-yo scene since she was eight. In fact, she won the U.S. National Championship in 1997.

"I was six and a half and on a family camping trip," she recalls. "One of the other campers had been a yo-yo demonstrator for the old Cheerio company. He was giving yo-yo lessons, and I just sort of picked it up. I started out with a Duncan Imperial."

Jennifer was a natural. By age eight, she had turned pro, getting paid to give demonstrations at libraries and recreation centers. And by age eleven, she was competing at the first world championships, finishing third to all the fifty-somethings who were yo-yo's superstars.

Jennifer graduated from Bellows Free Academy in St. Albans in 1998. She will devote herself full-time to yo-yo playing and teaching before going to college.

"I'm involved with a company called High Performance Marketing in Honolulu," she reports. "The boss, Alan Nagale, is a marketing genius. Our team took the first four places in the national championship in 1997. We're always finding great young talent in our training camp."

Most of the time, that talent is male. "I guess boys have more time to practice yo-yo," says Jennifer. "Girls are sort of closet yo-yo players."

What advice does the national champ have for youngsters starting out in yo-yo? "To be successful," she says, "you need to practice a lot, work hard, and, most important, have fun. And you don't need to start out with an expensive yo-yo. Something under ten dollars will do. The average yo-yo costs twenty dollars now. Some cost as much as a hundred dollars.

"The Yomega Brain was a major step forward in yo-yo making," says Jennifer. "With its built-in clutch, it could sleep for a long time."

Although there are one-handed and two-handed divisions in most yo-yo championships, the real champion is one who can use two hands at one time. "For me," says Jennifer, "my left hand does the straight out or looping tricks. My right hand does most of the work. Yo-yo became a lot better when freestyle competition came along. I have fun designing my routines, which, as in figure skating and gymnastics, are accompanied by music."

How does she come up with her three-minute routines? "First, I think of all my tricks. I know which ones I'll have to do to score with the judges. Harder tricks earn higher scores. I match the tricks to the music I've picked, and unlike most of the men, I add a few dance moves to my routine."

Jennifer loves to travel. Yo-yo has taken her lots of places, including eight trips to Japan for contests and demonstrations. And she's looking forward to her first trip to Korea.

THE COLLECTOR

Virtually every sport has a hall of fame containing historical souvenirs of the game. Yo-yo is no exception. The unofficial "keeper" in yo-yo is a dermatologist in Orlando, Florida. His name is Lucky Meisenheimer.

Lucky played with yo-yos as a kid, then picked them up seriously while in medical school. He has competed, though not at the level of the national masters. Instead, his big sport has always been swimming.

"Swimming gave me the opportunity to travel," he says. "And during one of my trips, I visited an antique store and found some old yo-yos. That got me started."

Now he owns more than 2,000 yo-yos. The rarest one in his collection is an experimental model made by Duncan for the Coca-Cola Company. "It's an all-white yo-yo, using Duncan's new (at that time) pearlescent paint," says Lucky. "Coke rejected the idea of putting its name on that yo-yo because their colors were red and white. Only six were made for the experiment, and it seems the other five have disappeared. So mine is one of a kind." Lucky has no idea what it's worth, but he's not about to sell it anyway!

However, even that yo-yo is not in the class of the yo-yo given to country singing legend Roy Acuff by Richard M. Nixon right before his resignation as president of the United States in 1974. Nixon used the yo-yo during an Acuff show at Nashville's Grand Ole Opry, then signed it and presented it to the star. Following Acuff's death, his estate packaged the yo-yo with a film of the presentation and auctioned it. It brought $16,029, the most ever spent on a yo-yo.

Lucky's oldest yo-yo is the original made by Pedro Flores in 1928. "That's the first use of the name yo-yo," he says. "Before that, yo-yos were called bandalores. And I've got some of them, too." He owns some unusual models, yo-yos that make sounds, bubbles, even sparks. He has some that fit on the ends of pencils. He collects string packs, the glassine envelopes that contained strings and were originally sold two for a nickel. And he owns yo-yo earrings, yo-yo bracelets, and other jewelry. "If it has something to do with yo-yo, I look for it."

Does Lucky see his collection being completed anytime soon? "No way," he says. "I'll never have them all, but I'll always be looking." In fact, he's now finishing the first really authoritative book on yo-yo collecting. "It has taken about four years, and I'm really pleased with it."

What does it take to be a yo-yo champion? According to Lucky Meisenheimer, skill, training, and a little bit of luck. "On any given day, any of the superstars may be number one," he says.

The biggest change in yo-yo these days? It's the Internet. "There are now so many sources of information," says Lucky. And it's easy to find all of the best sites. Bob of Bob's Land O' Yo catalogs them. You can log on with Bob at http://www.intergate.bc.ca/personal/Bobby/yo.html.

LEARNING MORE

Yo-yo is a great sport. Anyone can play. Unlike many sports, size plays no role in yo-yo. Neither does age. There are champs in their sixties and champs who haven't reached their teens.

There are few secrets. Football coaches never reveal their team's newest plays to anyone. Baseball managers have been known to have an extra pitcher warming up out of view. But yo-yoists are ready and eager to share their tips for success with anyone.

If you want to find out more about yo-yo, there are loads of ways to go. Yo-yo trick books are plentiful. With the current yo-yo boom, there should be an equal boom in your local bookstore. But you'll probably find an even better selection at yo-yo specialty stores. They're frequently located within big kite stores in your area.

More information about Dr. Lucky Meisenheimer's new book is available from Lucky at 7300 Sand Lake Commons Boulevard, Suite 105, Orlando, FL 32819.

Lucky is a member of the board of the American Yo-Yo Association. AYYA members include most of the major manufacturers, big collectors, players, and fans. You can join AYYA for as little as three dollars, though for just a little more you can also get a subscription to the AYYA newsletters. Discount subscriptions to the five-times-a-year *Yo-Yo Times* are also available. Write to the AYYA at 627 163rd Street South, Spanaway, WA 98387.

If you want to see how to do the tricks described here, your best bet may be a yo-yo video. Former world champ Dale Oliver has some great ones. Write to him at 439 Northwood Drive, San Francisco, CA 94080. Dale suggests following up with Dennis McBride's awesome videos. Write to Dennis at 2383 California Street, San Francisco, CA 94115.

Yo-yo manufacturers have always made instructional videos. For twenty dollars, Duncan will send you an Imperial yo-yo, strings, and a good video. Write Duncan at PO Box 5, Middlefield, OH 44062. Yomega, which makes great transaxle yo-yos, will send one — and a power spin video — for $23.45 including shipping and handling. Yomega Corp. is at PO Box 4146, Fall River, MA 02723. Don Duncan, Jr., son of the founder of Duncan Yo-Yo, has a fine one-hour video. Don, Jr., is with Playmaxx, 2900 North Country Club Road, Tucson, AZ 85716.

You can get good yo-yo instruction and a few laughs with the Smothers Brothers Yo-Yo Man Video. Comedian Tommy Smothers has long been the sport's unofficial spokesman and has used a yo-yo in his comedy act. Write to PO Box 789, Kenwood, CA 95452.

Another great source is the National Yo-Yo Museum in Chico, California. The head honcho is Bob Malowney, who directs the national championship tournament on the first weekend of every October. Bob is also the "greatest yo-yo announcer in the world," according to national master Dale Myrberg, who should know.

Finally, if you want instant information, the Internet is an incredible source. You can log onto the American Yo-Yo Association at http://www.pd.net/yoyo. Duncan has a terrific home page at http://www.kidshopon-line.com/duncan/index.html.

And these other sites have information on everything from buying and collecting yo-yos to perfecting the latest tricks:

http://members.aol.com/yoyotime/index.html
http://www.iwc.com/cosmicyo
http://www.yoyoing.com